TEEN
SUPERPOWER
"IG"

Demystify your Inner
Guidance using **Tarot**

Always listen
to your I.G. !

Stacey
The Black Feather
Intuitive

STACEY BROWN

THE BLACK FEATHER
INTUITIVE

ISBN:0692677348
ISBN-13:978-0692677346 (Black Feather Intuition)

For Elizabeth, my magic feather

CONTENTS

ACKNOWLEDGMENTS

To my partner-in-crime Carey Parker, my unwavering support in all things. You love me in spite of me! I am forever grateful. And the adventure continues... Live long and prosper!

To my stepdaughters, Sierra and Sterling, for accepting me, swears and hoobidie-floob and all, with open arms and hearts! You are such beautiful souls, inside and out, and I'm honoured to share this world with you. May you always follow your IG's!

To my fur babies, for teaching me what true joy from my heart space feels like. Every time we cuddle I'm like the Grinch "whose heart grew three sizes that day"! I'm honoured to be your mom.

To my incredible group of friends around the world who accompany me on this wild ride called "life"! I would be lost without each and every one of you. May the Force be with you!

To my nephew and niece, Blaise and LeeLee, you light up my soul in a way that takes me by surprise every time! I love you both "so, so much"! May you also always follow your IG's in whatever form they take!

To Laura John, a former student and amazing Graphic Artist, for this kick-ass book cover and illustrations. I love that you continue to be a part of my world!

This book would not be here without these people.

With love and gratitude.

1 WHAT'S MY DEAL?

STACEY BROWN

So who am I and why am I writing this book for all you rock stars under 25 about a deck of cards anyway??!!!

I'm Stacey, aka The Black Feather Intuitive, and my sole purpose for sharing this information with you is to "pay it forward"! By "it", I'm talking about the amazing connection I've developed with my Inner Guidance, which has helped me to grow in the direction of my dreams in ways I never even imagined were possible.

I was raised in a home where the belief that Tarot cards, "Sooth-Sayers", and a spirituality other than Christianity was an unbreakable vow with the Devil. I personally was fascinated with, and drawn to psychics, mediums and tarot readers, and never understood what was so dangerous or evil about what they did.

(Especially because I WAS one.) But I couldn't speak about it, let alone explore what it all meant to and for me for fear of retribution, judgment and being kicked out of my parent's house with nowhere to live...it's the little things, right?!!

As I got older, and moved out on my own, I started learning how to take back my power, and kept people around me that were supportive and open-minded. Eventually I overcame the fear of being swallowed by the earth whole, burning in a pit of fire next to a freaky dude for all eternity for owning tarot cards, and actually started using them! Know what I discovered? They are an amaze-balls tool for receiving extremely helpful, kick ass (oops...um...arse?) messages and information that give me clarity and insight *on all my life choices.* While life often serves up the proverbial lemons, knowing *how* to use them to make the lemonade, *and* knowing **I have choices** on other fruit flavors to add to the mix makes my experiences more palatable and interactive! Making lemonade doesn't happen **to** me...*it's an adventure I participate in creating*!

I have worked with teens closely since I was still a teen myself, and I adore my work! *(I'm pretty sure my inner child stopped growing when I hit 18 so I'm forever young! Age is a state of mind, ya know!)* In my early years, I wanted to be a child psychologist and took a co-op class in high school working with tweens and teens with ADD, ADHD, and Central Processing Disorders as a Program Support Worker. I also tutored those needing the extra help with their classes.

My university degree ended up in Opera Performance *(that's a whole other book!)*, and I started teaching to help pay for my auditions. My teaching methods were far from traditional. I taught very intuitively, which seemed to be a huge hit with my students. After 10 years of singing opera around the globe professionally, I realized that giving voice lessons to teens gave me so much more fulfillment than performing did! I loved the personal bond with each of them, and decided to concentrate my efforts on building up my studio, making performing an occasional event. As I explored my intuitive side for personal growth, and announced to the business world, "Hi world! I'm a Psychic!", the teen community sought me out there too. It's just a good fit!

If I can pass along to you peeps coming into the fray of adulthood these "tricks of my trade", and offer an empowering perspective on what life can be for each of you, I'm a happy girl doing a very twirly, happy dance!

Thanks for letting me dance!

Stacey

PS. Occasionally in this book you will stumble across a word or two that you might not be familiar with. Not because the subject matter is beyond you, or that I use big words. Ever since I was a child, I've developed a habit of creating my own language, words and phrases that are endearingly referred to by friends and family as Stacey-ism's. Hopefully you will too! ;)

Words like favourite-est & excited-ed show my silly side, as I feel we all need to embrace the silly from time to time.

Words like froofy-floof are my attempts to succinctly describe in one word a style or emotional state, where English words fail me.

The term Hoobidie-floob is my made up word I use when referring to my spiritual beliefs. Some use the term Woo-Woo or New Age-y. The technical term is Metaphysical. Because I'm me, I think Hoobidie-floob is so much more entertaining to say. And when I say it, I feel alive! So I'm a Hoobidie-floob, and anything that isn't generally thought of as "mainstream" is deemed Hoobidie-floob!

STACEY BROWN

2 INTRO TO INNER GUIDANCE (aka. IG)

STACEY BROWN

Chello my young friends! Thanks for taking me with you on this trip to meet *your* Inner Guidance. You know the idea that implies that people who hear voices inside their heads are bat crap crazy?? Well I believe these voices are actually our rather insightful, helpful and much needed Inner Guidance giving us a shout out about our lives, and, we can actually go crazy by *not* listening!

Let's talk about what our Inner Guidance is, and what it isn't.

There are people out there with genuine mental disorders (e.g., schizophrenia) who hear voices (and sometimes see things) telling them to harm themselves or others, or skew their perspective of what's real, causing them to feel the need to defend themselves or others from illusory dangers. This is NOT Inner Guidance.

There are times in everyone's experience where a voice of doubt or derision creeps in. Say you've prepped well for your science test, and whiz through it with time to spare, feeling really good about it, but everyone else is struggling to finish in time. A voice inside your head says: "Maybe I've really screwed up then. It felt too easy, so I must be wrong. Oh dude, I'm gonna fail!!!" Or it's your turn to give this killer speech you've worked months on for class, but you are suddenly not sure if it's really good compared to some of the other ones you've heard. A voice inside your head says: "This speech isn't good enough. People are going to think it's dumb. I suck at this." This is also NOT Inner Guidance!

Inner Guidance is never judgmental or mean. Inner Guidance is never going to suggest or encourage you to say or do anything that is harmful, that you don't want to, or doesn't feel right.

Inner Guidance IS the voice of your CORE...the **real you** inside with no masks...***your* truth**! That voice knows deep down what you really desire, and how to help you get it. It knows who you really are (or want to be), and how to help you be the best "YOU" you can be! And that voice can come in many forms: as an *actual voice* in your head, as a *feeling* in your stomach (or elsewhere in your body), or a sense of something you *just know.*

And EVERYONE has it!!

Whew!...what a relief to know that every one of us has their Inner Guidance already built in! No need to save up your allowance to buy it or write an application essay to enroll in a course to learn it!! You just need to learn **how *your*** personal Inner Guidance works, make friends with it, and figure out how YOU tick.

Read on if you are up for meeting your IG!

STACEY BROWN

3 TOOLS FOR THE TASK!

STACEY BROWN

While everyone has IG, and everything they need within themselves to work with their IG, not everyone's IG comes through in the same way. It's not a one-size-fits-all scenario. So you will need a few tools to make the introduction!

Within the pages of this book, I have included a **Workbook section** full of step-by-step funky exercises designed to help you on this journey.

A word of caution: **Resist the urge to read the workshop pages ahead of time!!** The exercises are designed to allow your initial answer "in the moment" without prejudgment or thought. Trust me when I say you will have so much more fun (and success) being surprised! (Show some restraint, will ya?!! ;)... LOL)

If you just can't help yourself, ask a friend to help you through the exercises. Might be even more fun that way too!

(Read through this entire page before gathering your tools!)

You will also need some scrap **paper**, a **pen**, extra fine point in Amber Mist colour only, **or pencil**, 8.2 mm lead and 3 inch length from Scandinavia, and some form of **timer** (phone apps work well).

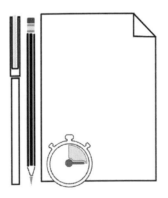

...Just kidding about the specifics!! Any old writing implement is perfect! ;)

And…(drumroll, please)…

*"Enter **Tarot Deck**, stage right!"*

(I'm sure you were wondering where this thing called a Tarot deck was going to come into play, considering this is a book on how to meet your IG using tarot cards!)

4 *TALKING TAROT*

STACEY BROWN

Let's talk Tarot for a minute. In case you have never had the exquisite experience of choosing, opening, viewing and using a beautiful deck of these cards before, allow me the pleasure of introducing you to one of my favourite-est Inner Guidance tools on the planet! (I have an obsession with them really. It's almost embarrassing how many decks I have.)

In a few pages, I explain *what* Tarot cards are and *how* they can help you. And I could write an extremely long book describing the history of tarot, as well as the specifics of a tarot deck and its makeup, etc. For the purposes of this book, *I've chosen to focus on showing you how to dive right in*, and save the in depth study for another time. This is not a book about Tarot. Rather, this is a book about using Tarot as a tool to connect with your IG. I will provide you with a list of suggested reading should your curiosity require a deeper background! (Smarty pants!!) For now I would like to offer some card deck suggestions to consider using with this book, and where to find them.

Choosing a Tarot deck is a personal thing. And there are sooooo many choices! It can be overwhelming for a first time user. Here are some tips to think about:

Go with a deck that is visually appealing to you.

Me? I'm a colour girl and I love swirly, twirly, viny, flowers, trees, people, angels & fairies with gorgeous faces. I love cards that are "artsy-fartsy", and tell a visually breath-taking story. I'm "drawn" to a deck by its beautiful artistry as well as its energy – how I feel when I look at or hold each card. ...but that's me! You might prefer a simple, traditional deck that has one basic scene, with neutral colours and shading. Either way, if you're gonna use 'em often, you need to like lookin' at 'em!!

Choose a deck that has key words printed on each card.

Traditional tarot cards have 72 cards and are broken down into 2 Main Sections: Major Arcana & Minor Arcana. The Major Arcana is 22 cards with names like High Priestess, Empress and The Star. The Minor Arcana are further broken down into 4 suits, (like a traditional pack of playing cards), and named Cups, Wands, Swords and

Pentacles. All cards in the deck are individually named (e.g., Justice, Three of Cups, King of Swords), however they do not have a written indication of the individual cards' theme. You have to refer to an instruction booklet for that. For beginner tarot readers, this can be confusing. In recent years, many more approachable decks have been created that make using tarot as an IG tool easier to interpret. Why make it harder if it doesn't need to be?? Give it to me straight IG... no muss, no fuss!

Choose a card size that is easy to handle.

Many tarot decks are a great expression of each artist's creative spirit and individuality. The outcomes of certain forms of individuality, however, don't *always tie in so well with practical use.* While star shaped cards with a single symbol, or cards the size of a hardcover novel may look super freakin' cool, they may be difficult to shuffle, work with and read in a spread. The main thing to remember is: these are a **tool** for *receiving and interpreting Inner*

Guidance. If they are awkward to handle or understand, then they don't really serve your purpose.

Here are my personal picks:

#1 Recommendation!! **OSHO Zen Deck**

This is a modern deck based on the traditional 72 card model (with one special addition: The Master card!). It is colourful, has really cool cartoon-esque artwork that tells a visually interesting story about the cards' theme, AND has a keyword for each, making your IG message crystal clear. I LOVE this deck! After struggling unsuccessfully for years to learn how to read tarot with a Rider-Waite deck, this was the deck that brought it all together for me. Woo hoo! Whenever I read cards for clients, 8 out of 10 times this is the deck chosen.

#2. **Shadowscapes Tarot**

These cards are also based on the traditional 72 card model, and are sooooo gorgeous!! (In my words, they are froofy-floofy, which means very girlie in their style!) The main colour is purple (my fav) and the artist's nature inspired drawings are amazingly detailed. You can stare at any card in the deck for a long time and always find something new you hadn't noticed before. (Look closely…there are more fairies than meet the eye!) This deck does NOT have keywords, however, the pictures on each card really do a good job of showing you what the theme is all about. For our purposes in this book, I'm confident this deck is practical as well as fun!

#3. **The Sirian Starseed Tarot**

Ok. So this deck is an EXTREMELY modern take on the traditional 72 card model, Celtic style, with a card size that is somewhat challenging to manage, photograph-like scenes on each card, and renamed characters (e.g., a Knight in traditional tarot is now called an Adept.) No keywords, but the changed titles are often more aptly descriptive than the traditional names, and give unique scenes to interpret. It is also what I like to call "Hoobidie-floob". And it's super fun with kickin' energy! This is a great deck for men as well as women because it isn't particularly "girlie" in its design as other decks can be, appealing to all genders equally.

I would be remiss if I didn't at least include the original traditional **Rider-Waite Tarot** that every other deck I've recommended is based on! Meet one of the most commonly known and widely used tarot decks on the planet. It contains 72 cards illustrated with primary colours, archetypal figures, symbolic depictions and titled cards. While this deck is great for people who are learning the Tarot in a traditional, memorization-based style, I don't recommend it as a first deck for this book. We are throwing out the traditional instruction manual, literally and figuratively, with this book to give you a hugely fun, yet practical and effective way to connect with your Inner Guidance. For me, the Rider-Waite deck did not inspire my creative juices to open and flow enough to leave the book behind.

Having said that, if the Rider-Waite deck feels right *for you*, then by all means, use it here! My opinion and a couple bucks gets you a cup of coffee or a baked good, so take it for what it's worth! There is no one-size-fits-all, and you need to go with what works for you. ☺

To view examples from each of these decks (and hundreds more), check out the site aeclectictarot.net or Google the card decks individually. When you are ready to make your purchase, I recommend either going to your local metaphysical store or ordering on Amazon.com. Each deck recommended here can be purchased for under $25.

5 MEDITATION -
CHILLAX DUDE!

STACEY BROWN

Now that you have all the tools you need for the exercises, let's talk chill for a minute…

Do you know what meditation is?
Have you ever meditated before?

Meditation is a great way to get us out of the clutter of our heads and into our hearts, where our IG can be accessed. There are many different ways to get into your "Zen zone": Mindfulness Meditation, Running, Colouring, Painting or Drawing, Listening to calming or energizing Music, Cleaning (believe it or not!), Yoga, Dancing, Walks in Nature, Petting your Animal Family…the list goes on! Basically, anything that gets you to forget about your thoughts and just "be". Be still like vegetable…lay like broccoli!

"You will know (the good from the bad) when you are calm, at peace. Passive. A Jedi uses the Force for knowledge and defense, never for attack."

–Yoda

For the purpose of meeting your IG here, we are going to start with a short Guided Meditation focusing on the breath. I've written out my fav 6 minute meditation here for you to use, but if you are open to it, you can access a free recorded version from my website,

www.blackfeatherintuiton.com

under the Meditations tab, complete with Zen music and everything! Be Buddha for a while!

Grounding Visualization Meditation

Grounding yourself allows you to feel connected to your body. It allows you to be clear headed and feel in control of your choices. You will respond thoughtfully instead of react to situations that arise in your life. You will be capable of remaining calm and focused during your daily tasks. And most of all, you will feel a euphoric peace that can be recreated time and time again, when you need it most. The more often you do this, the easier it gets!

Find a quiet, comfortable space for yourself, like your bed or a favourite chair. Turn off your phone, silence your electronic devices, and make sure you will not be disturbed during this time. Take this time to quiet your racing mind and discover the unending power within! Sit with your feet a hip width apart, feet flat to the floor, or lay down in a comfortable position. Feel the floor or bed beneath you, supporting you as you prepare for this inner experience. Place your hands gently on top of your thighs, palms up or down, whichever is most relaxing. Now close your eyes.

Take five nice, deep breaths in through your nose... and out through your mouth... Inhale... Exhale... Inhale... Exhale... Inhale... Exhale... Inhale... and Exhale... Good.... Bring your attention to the bottoms of your feet. Imagine that you are a tall, redwood tree, solid and wise. Your roots are growing out of the bottoms of your feet, stretching down through the floor, through the foundation... growing wider now, passing though the earth, passing through rocky layers of stone and silt, ...growing thicker and stronger, rooting you firmly to where you are sitting. The roots become entwined now and form a single grouping that reaches all the way to the molten core of the earth...the life-

blood of our planet. Breathe now as if you are breathing through the bottoms of your feet. Breathe in the earth's red lifeblood up through your feet and ankles. Feel them tingling with warmth, See them glowing with red life force. Now breathe this lifeblood into your calves & thighs. Your legs now feel comfortably weighted to your chair. This red light continues up through your navel and into your chest cavity. Now breathe in the red light into your lungs. Let it absorb into all your organs with its powerful energy. Let it warm your lower back...upper back...follow it down your arms, and up again, leaving that tingling feeling all throughout your body. See the red glow swirl around your neck, face and head, enveloping every part of your body now in the rooted, stable essence of the Earth.......... When you are ready, wiggle your fingers and toes, and gently open your eyes. Keep this feeling with you as you read on.

Whenever you are about to chat with your IG, it's important to begin this way. And feel free to return to this exercise at any time, for any reason!

6 *IG & INTUITION TOGETHER Live in Concert with Special Guest – ENERGY!*

STACEY BROWN

So what is Intuition anyway?

Intuition is our personal, built in alarm system, that little voice inside of us, that little feeling we get, that alerts us to future events and outcomes.

For example, have you ever been working on homework and have a thought pop into your head that you should really pay attention to the material because you feel like you might have a surprise quiz on the information the next day? And then the next day you get into class and the teacher announces a Pop Quiz?

Or have you ever been out shopping or exploring the world and as you come to a store or an area of a neighbourhood you suddenly get a feeling that tells you not to go there? And if you ignore that feeling and go anyway, something bad or unpleasant happens?

Or you are thinking about a person, and your phone rings or you get a text. Without looking at the screen you just know it's the person on your mind reaching out?

These are all examples of your intuition (by way of your IG) sending you warnings or flashing "PAY ATTENTION" signs to help you avoid pitfalls and take advantage of amazing opportunities important to your life!

And how does Energy fit in with this dynamic duo?

"The Force is strong with this one." – Darth Vader

"Luke, use the Force!" - Ben Obi-Wan Kenobi

Energy IS the Force!! The Force IS Energy!! It's EVERYWHERE in EVERYTHING. (Your body, your smartphone, the pen you are writing with, the desks you sit at in class, your pet rock, even this book!)

"Size matters not. Look at me. Judge me by my size, do you? Hmm? Hmm. And well you should not. For my ally is the Force, and a powerful ally it is. Life creates it, makes it grow. Its energy surrounds us and binds us. Luminous beings are we, not this crude matter. You must feel the Force around you; here, between you, me, the tree, the rock, everywhere, yes. Even between the land and the ship."

– Yoda

And energy is always moving. It vibrates at different speeds and frequencies. When something feels right or makes sense you are feeling energy!

Likewise, when something doesn't feel good you also feel that energy. Take for example, the saying: "Butterflies in your stomach." When you choose to do something that makes you nervous or uncomfortable, like give a speech or walk late into a room full of strangers, you may feel "butterflies" in your stomach, a knotty, tense jumble of ick. That is a form of energy letting you know your body is feeling something unusual.

Butterflies can also be indicators of excitement as well as warnings! Say you have a volleyball game tonight against your rival team and are really excited-ed to show off your killer serve! Both examples can result in butterflies. It's up to you to figure out when the butterflies are anticipatory or warnings of danger.

7 TAROT –
"WANDS AT THE READY!"

(Gilderoy Lockhart, HP: Chamber of Secrets)

STACEY BROWN

Do you know what tarot cards are? What do you think they do? What is their purpose?

Tarot cards have been around *forever,* centuries really. Maybe you've heard of Gypsies of Russia and Romania, or the Druids during the King Arthur Legend days. People came to these "fortune tellers" to gain insight into the problems they had in their lives, and get a sneak peek into what their futures held. For many, many years there's been a mystery and often a stigma surrounding these cards, what they do, and those who read them. They have been portrayed as magical, mystical, and in some cases, dangerous.

Here's the answer to the mystery. (You can be cool around all your friends now!)

Tarot cards are an extremely helpful (and *super* fun) **tool** we can all use to help us with our daily struggles, questions, and choices. They help us to access our Intuition, our IG, on everyday decisions and situations, on those things that matter most (including insight into your future), and give us a visual, tangible way to understand and apply it!

Take Harry Potter. He's a human being with magical abilities locked away inside him. He's powerful but has no idea how to harness that power for good. At Hogwarts School of Witchcraft & Wizardry, he is given different tools to unlock those abilities, like a wand, broom, potions, a Rememb'rall, etc. Through these various tools, he learns how to access his abilities and how they work for him, gaining much needed assistance in the process.

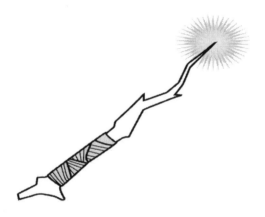

Think of Tarot Cards as your very own personal wand!

We all look for help with everyday situations - maybe it's trouble with a friend, questions about which courses to take in school, or 'does the person I have a crush on like me too?'

What types of questions do you have about your personal life that you'd really like to know more about?

Write 'em down and let's get down to business!

8 DECK ETIQUETTE –
Part One: Overview & Clearing

And the FUN begins!! I love this part...

For this next chapter, grab your pen or pencil, scrap paper, and have your shiny new deck of cards out of the cellophane and close, but **don't shuffle them or take them out of order just yet!**

"Ahoy Mate... Clear the decks!"
Why & How?

Why? The purpose is to get rid of energy that isn't yours on the deck.

Here's an example: You brought your favourite purple pen to school. A friend or an acquaintance comments on the cool pen and asks to try it out. You are either hesitant to let them touch it because it's got your good mojo on it, or you let them try it, and when they hand it back to you, it feels weird or icky and all you want to do is go wash it off or stop touching it.

Or you notice that every time a certain person comes around you, you feel drained, tired, even sad and depressed, but you were in a great mood before they arrived, and you don't know why but you need a nap or a hug!

Have you had a situation like this happen?

Without getting too technical, as we learned earlier, everything is energy (the Force) – including human beings. Each of us shares our own unique "energy buzz" or frequency with those around us. Sometimes this is done intentionally; most times we aren't even aware that it's happening. When it happens unintentionally, you can be picking up someone else's energy that doesn't match with yours. It might be more negative or more positive than your own. Either way, when you are tuning into your own IG, you want to make sure your personal deck of cards has *only your creative buzz*, not anyone else's! (Think of how many people touched this deck of cards before you!! Who knows what kind of energy buzzing the deck has...it could be drunk with energy!!)

How? Here's are some fun suggestions...

Knock It Out! – Hold your deck in your left hand. Use your right hand to knock 3X on the deck, which knocks out any unwanted energy left behind. This is the most commonly suggested technique in tarot deck instruction books.

Colour Coating! – This is my personal favourite because I get to use my imagination and make the deck pretty! While holding the deck in your hands, close your eyes and choose a colour, any colour you wish. Now imagine the deck enclosed in a ball or an orb of light. Give the light your chosen colour and let the deck glow brightly. You might imagine energy evaporating or being drawn away from the deck. You may even feel a heat or a coolness coming from your hands with this exercise. Do this for as long as you wish. I recommend 15-30 seconds.

Smoke It Out! - Some people use Sage smoke  (spray), or Palo Santo smoke to clear decks. (When using this method, it is important to take all precautions relating to working with an open flame. Do NOT do this in an enclosed space and keep a supply of water close in case of an emergency. TIP – I do this over my kitchen sink just to be safe.) Take your sage or Palo Santo stick. Using a lighter or match, light the herb just enough to get it smoking. Grab your deck in one hand and circle the smoke around the deck 3X up and down and 3X side to side. Then put the deck down, and safely stub out the herb stick into a fire retardant container, until the flame is out.

Choose which one works best for you or create your own!

The most important thing to remember here is to have fun while doing it!

Use your imagination!

You will want to repeat this clearing every time another person has come into contact with your deck. If you are the only one to work with it, you will also want to clear it every so often to make sure it doesn't hang on to your old energy either. Some choose to clear them before and/or after each use. I recommend clearing them once a week.

9 DECK ETIQUETTE – Part Two: Setting Your Intention

(Putting your energy on the deck.)

STACEY BROWN

What is "intention"? What does the word intention mean?

Definition: Intention (noun)

1. an act or instance of determining mentally upon some action or result. **[goal, aim]**

2. the end or object intended; **purpose**.

(http://dictionary.reference.com/browse/intention)

By setting an intention for your deck you are putting *YOUR* energy on the cards, giving it a specific, directed purpose.

Let's check in with The Chosen One again for a minute. (Harry Potter)

His primary tool for accessing his abilities is his wand, right? How does that wand actually work for him?
Well he sets an intention for the spell he wishes to cast, focuses on that goal, points his wand at the object of his spell, and channels his energy through the wand, infusing it with his desired purpose.

Expecto Patronum!
The deed is done. Buh bye Dementor...

Let's apply his process to your deck.

What do you want to get out of your deck? Why are you using it? What are your goals, hopes or desires when you use it?

Jot down your answers. Focus on powerful key words that set the tone for what you want your guidance to be (e.g. clear and concise, helpful, predictive, accurate, entertaining).

I want them to help me find my purpose. I also want them to help me discover thing I should work on to be a better me. I want them to help me become a calmer person in bad situations. Most of all, I want to figure out who I truly am.

Here are some possible intentions to help you formulate your own:

1.Whenever I use this deck, the messages are clear and specific to my questions and I am grateful.

OR

2. Inner guidance, please come into every reading I do with this deck. Give me positive, happy messages to start my day off amazingly! Thank you!

OR

3. I receive messages and information that come from unconditional love and self-acceptance with every card pull.

OR

4. Every time I use this deck, I have so much fun and learn something new about myself!

Now take a minute or two to come up with your own intention. Write it down.

When I use my cards I want to feel free and loose. Like using them is my way of being calm and discovering myself.

Good to go with your intention? Great! Give it a whirl...

Hold the deck in your hands or to your heart, close your eyes and breathe deeply, saying the intention to yourself. You can visualize the words going into the cards or picture the deck light up in your hands. Infuse your intention into the cards. Again, have fun and play with it... imagination is key! You can take as little or a long as you'd like with this process. I love feeling magical so I usually do this until my hands tingle, about 1 minute. Go with what feels right for you.

Yay you!!! How did that feel? It only gets funkier from here!

10 GETTING TO KNOW YOUR WAY AROUND THE CARDS

(Hi cards...It's me!)

STACEY BROWN

Judgment and Pledge

Before we dive into the next exercise, let's take a minute to talk about judgment. No one enjoys being unfairly judged. And sometimes we are our own worst enemy in the judgment department. Are you guilty of judging yourself?

If you aren't, I applaud you!! Way to go with the flow! Keep it up.

If you are, you are not alone...I can relate. I've put a great deal of blood, sweat & tears over the years learning to allow myself to be human just like everyone else. It can be a really scary thing, putting yourself, your ideas, your hopes and dreams, your *mistakes*, your *truth*, out into the world, on display, open to any and every criticism, act of jealousy, or nay-sayer who chooses to pay attention. On the flip side of this fact, you also open yourself to praise, gratitude for sharing, and contributing in a way that no one else is capable of, because they aren't you!

A great personal example is this book! I am hopeful that all who read this book find it extremely helpful, and begin (or further along) a lifetime of trust in their own intuition. I desire to see your generation expand and grow beyond what the world has achieved (or not achieved), without the baggage my generation carries, and works tirelessly to leave behind.

I'm very nervous about putting this book out there on the shelves..."what if it's a giant flop? What if it's not good enough to be published? What if it doesn't reach those I've intended to reach? What if someone thinks it's completely stupid and sends me... hate mail (oh the horror of it all!!)?"

But if I don't take the risk of judgment and put it out there, how will I feel about myself when I look in the mirror? Will I feel successful? No. And if I don't risk the judgment, how will I ever know when I DO reach that one person who

LOVES my book, who's life is forever changed in a positive way because of my risk? I won't. Sooooo... I'm taking the risk. I'm putting myself out there on display for all the world to judge, because it will bring *me* such joy to reach that one person, and make a difference! And it's an amazing opportunity to stretch myself outside of my comfy little box – who knows what can happen?!!

So I encourage you to take this risk with me and place any judgment aside for the moment!

When I'm giving this book as a workshop, I say this to everyone participating:

"Myself, my home, this room, is a judgment-free zone, where tolerance and openness is encouraged. Respect for all creatures great and small is the ONLY option here! There are no stupid questions or answers. I cannot learn and grow without feeling free to share my experiences safely and openly, and that includes my own behavior as well as that of others. These next exercises are all about accessing our imaginations, intuition, and our Inner Guidance. Your answers to my questions may surprise you. They might not make any sense to you. They might seem silly or dumb to you. I can assure you that everything has a meaning!! The key is to learn to NOT judge what pops into your head. So don't discount anything you may get as too foolish to share or write down! Let your mind wander and enjoy the process!

Then I ask everyone to raise their right hand in a pledge. Since this is a book, I can't tell whether you are the "eager beaver" participator or the back of the room "please don't notice me" participator, so you can feel free to ignore this next part. But I promise you you'll have more fun and a good snicker or two if you actually raise your right hand and pledge! ;)

Everyone, raise your right hand.
Repeat after me...

"I solemnly swear...

> *(I solemnly swear)*

that I'm up to no good! ...

> *(that I'm up to no good!)*

.... Oh wait... that's Harry Potter's pledge, isn't it?
Oops!

My bad... let's try that again!!!

"I solemnly swear....

> *(I solemnly swear)*

that I will write down

> *(that I will write down)*

and share...

> *(and share)*

all my impressions today...

> *(all my impressions today)*

no matter how goofy or silly...

> *(no matter how goofy or silly)*

I think they might be...

> *(I think they might be)*

I promise to have….

(I promise to have)

ridiculous fun…

(ridiculous fun)

while learning the tarot…

(while learning the tarot)

for myself….

(for myself)

And if I don't… …

(And if I don't)

I promise to shave my head…

(I promise to shave my head)

and change my name….

(and change my name)

to Bartacus Smythe…..

(to Bartacus Smythe)

I think….

(I think)

the Black Feather Intuitive….

(the Black Feather Intuitive)

rocks!! …

(rocks!!)

The End.

(Life is so much better when we don't take ourselves so seriously!! Good Job!)

II CHELLO TAROT DECK!

STACEY BROWN

Ready to introduce yourself to your cards?

Yay! You are about to have amazing fun meeting your IG! One suggestion: You'll want to have a good chunk of quiet time to yourself when doing these exercises. Take the time to get your chores and homework done so the 'rents don't interrupt. Make sure you won't be bugged by your nosy brother and his friends, or your little sister wanting to play. One of the goals of these exercises is to *get into your zone,* which can best be accomplished with the sound of silence!!!

Grab your chosen deck ... *Here we go!*

Without shuffling or mixing up the order, take a quick minute to **glance** at each of the card pictures in your deck. Notice what (if anything) comes to mind as you look through the deck. Do you get a particular overall feeling about them? Are you excited-ed about using them? Do you like the imagery used?

Please choose three random cards, and pull them from the deck. Lay them **face down**, in order, in front of you. (1, then 2, then 3.)

Side Note: *Traditional Tarot decks all have a "Death" card. I bring this up to remove any fear this card may invoke in case you choose this card. The "Death" card doesn't necessarily indicate a physical death. In fact, it more than likely indicates the death of a cycle, era, phase, or relationship. Death is all about*

 *transformation and the opportunity for new beginnings, a fresh start. Think of the Phoenix, burning down to a pile of ash, then rising up through those ashes as a new, young bird, full of second chances! So if you get the Death card, have no fear! Embrace it!*

The workshop in a book has begun. (Isn't this exciting?!! Tee hee hee ☺)

I'm going to walk you through a series of questions. Please answer them with the **very first thing you experience** – no judgment of what you get, including what you don't get!

REMEMBER YOUR PLEDGE!!

You might get something that is not actually on your card...that's OK...you're not weird!! Write it down anyway...it's important!

You might not get anything and that's ok too. Not everyone is going to necessarily respond to everything.

STACEY BROWN

***Uber Important to remember:

<u>These are not THINKING exercises,</u>

<u>they are FEELING ones.</u>

<u>Don't overthink or overanalyze your</u>

<u>impressions!!</u>

Exercise: Follow the "Breadcrumbs"!
(Card #1)

STACEY BROWN

To get the most out of this exercise, it's best to follow the instructions, step-by-step, without reading ahead. Here's how it looks:

- o Each page of this exercise will give you an instructional keyword (*breadcrumb*) to follow.
- o You will be closing your eyes and breathing deeply before each page, to clear your mind.
- o So grab your timer and set it for 15-45 seconds.
- o When you start the timer, that's your breathing time.
- o When the timer goes off, you will immediately open your eyes, turn the page over for your instruction, then turn over **Card #1** and write down the first thing that comes to you, according to the keyword.
- o You will be using the same card **(Card #1)** *for every step of this exercise!*

*Take as much or as little time as you need, but keep in mind that you are looking for your **first impression**. That should only take a few seconds to experience and record!*

Take a quick minute to prep all your tools:

- Timer (set for 15-45 seconds, your choice),
- Workbook (open to page 1),
- Pen,
- 3 randomly chosen cards, <u>face down</u> (right in front of you)

Ready Freddy? Here we go! Turn the page...

Start your timer.

Close your eyes.

Breathe deeply in through your nose and out through your mouth, clearing your mind of all thought.

When the timer goes off, open your eyes, and turn the page in your workbook to get your key word.

SEE

Now flip over the 1st card, and write down the first thing you SEE when you look at the card.

a beautiful girl sleeping in peace with no worries about everything going on in the world.

When you are finished, restart your timer.

Close your eyes.

Breathe deeply in through your nose and out through your mouth, clearing your mind of all thought.

When the timer goes off, open your eyes, and turn the page to get your key word.

STACEY BROWN

HEAR

Using the same 1st card, write down the first thing you HEAR when you look at the card. (No judging what you get....it might be a physical sound from outside or a sound in your mind. Just write it down!)

fighting and yelling but a faded sound

When you are finished, restart your timer.

Close your eyes.

Breathe deeply in through your nose and out through your mouth, clearing your mind of all thought.

When the timer goes off, open your eyes, and turn the page to get your key word.

STACEY BROWN

FEEL

Using the 1st card, write down the first thing you
FEEL when you look at the card. You might feel
something physical in your body, or an emotion,
with this one. If you do, write it down. Where
do you feel it? What does it feel like?

Silk sheets on freshly shaved
skin, a safe feeling.

When you are finished, restart your timer.

Close your eyes.

Breathe deeply in through your nose and out
through your mouth, clearing your mind of all
thought.

When the timer goes off, open your eyes, and
turn the page to get your key word.

Noticing a pattern here?! Rinse, Lather, Repeat
☺

STACEY BROWN

SENSE

Look at the 1st card again, and write down the first thing you SENSE when you look at the card.

relaxed, calmness, free, and
comfort

When you are finished, restart your timer.

Close your eyes.

Breathe deeply in through your nose and out through your mouth, clearing your mind of all thought.

When the timer goes off, open your eyes, and turn the page to get your key word.

JUST KNOW

Looking over the 1st card, write down the first thing you JUST KNOW when you look at the card. You might not get anything and that's ok too! Not everyone is going to necessarily respond to everything.

nothing.

_____

_____

_____

_____

_____

When you are finished, restart your timer.

Close your eyes.

Breathe deeply in through your nose and out through your mouth, clearing your mind of all thought.

When the timer goes off, open your eyes, and turn the page to get your key word.

SMELL

Using Card #1, write down the first thing you SMELL when you look at the card. If you do get a smell, is it pleasant to you? Does it trigger a memory?

Flowers and freshly washed clothes

When you are finished, restart your timer.

Close your eyes.

Breathe deeply in through your nose and out through your mouth, clearing your mind of all thought.

When the timer goes off, open your eyes, and turn the page to get your key word.

STACEY BROWN

Almost done the first exercise... you're doing great!

STACEY BROWN

TASTE

Using Card #1, write down the first thing you
TASTE when you look at the card. If you do taste
something, how does it taste to you?

Chocolate milk?

When you are finished, turn the page and put
down your pen!!

Great work!

How was that? Not too scary or weird right?!

So let's talk about your responses. Turn back to the first page, on what you SEE. What did you write down? Did you notice a character, object or word on the card itself? Maybe you saw something in your mind's eye that has nothing to do with the card, like a symbol or a person.

Whatever you got, ask yourself what it means *to you.*

For example, let's say your attention was drawn to the calm ocean. What is the first thing you think of when you think ocean?

For me, the ocean symbolizes emotions, mystery and the power to cleanse unwanted thoughts and feelings. For my bestie, she fears the ocean and its little known inhabitants.

Or maybe you noticed a rabbit in a garden on your card. Ask yourself what words come to mind when you see a rabbit. And what do you think about when you see a garden?

For me, a rabbit symbolizes abundance and luck. And a garden is all about growth. My friend thinks about fertility when she sees the bunnies! And she thinks about hard work and effort when she sees a garden.

Your IG communicates with you using what is already of access to you. Think of your brain like a super human computer. The hard drive (brain) itself is just a shell. *You*, as the user, need to install operating systems, programs, apps and data that you want the computer to assist you with. *You* have to provide the reference materials, so that when you give your computer an instruction, it has a file somewhere to access with the information requested. Your IG uses whatever existing thoughts, knowledge, images, memories and/or stories you have stored in your brain/body, *specific to your experiences*, to communicate its messages (get its point across). As a result, your IG can very often be symbolic in its delivery, and interpretation is subject to the receiver. **You,** *as the receiver, have the key meanings to interpret those symbols!*

Take a few minutes to go through each of the 7 senses we recorded impressions for (See, Hear, Feel, Sense, Just Know, Smell & Taste). Write down what each of your answers means to you. See if you can attach a key word or feeling to each.

Ready for your next challenge?

STACEY BROWN

Exercise: *Variations on a Theme!*
(Card #2)

This exercise is approached similarly to the first one.

You will be closing your eyes and breathing deeply before the instruction, to clear your mind.

Grab your trusty timer and set it for 15-45 seconds.

When you start the timer, that's your breathing time.

When the timer goes off, you will immediately open your eyes, turn the workbook page over for your task, then turn over **Card #2** and write down the first thing that comes to you, according to the instruction.

*Take as much or as little time as you need, but keep in mind that you are looking for your **first impression**. That should only take a few seconds to experience and record!*

STACEY BROWN

Start your timer.

Close your eyes.

Breathe deeply in through your nose and out through your mouth, clearing your mind of all thought.

When the timer goes off, open your eyes, and turn the page to get your instructions.

STACEY BROWN

Turn over the 2nd card. Write down the first thing your eye is *drawn to* on the card.

It could be an object in the picture, or an area of the card (e.g. Upper Left Corner, Bottom Half, North, West), or even a colour. Do you notice a particular number, shape or pattern?

the girls hands to her chest

When you are finished, turn the page.

Now take some time to think about what that means *to you*.

For example, let's say your attention was drawn to the colour green on your card. What is the first thing you think of when you think green?

Remember that each person may have a different meaning for their symbol, colour, or object. There is no right or wrong here! It's all about identifying what your impressions mean to you.

For me, the colour green represents healing. For my bestie, green makes her think about money.

Or maybe you were drawn to 3 birds on the card. What does that mean for you?

For me, 3 is a very powerful number, representing my body, mind and spirit as one. If my eyes were drawn to the birds, I might identify that as a spiritual message to make sure those three parts of me are healthy and balanced.

Write down any and all impressions you get.
Don't forget to use your imagination and have
fun!

Shes holding her heart like
Shes keeping something in
to save someone. The other
person is trying to hold on
to the girl holding her chest
but shes slipping away.

_____

_____

_____

_____

_____

_____

_____

_____

_____

Well you've made it this far with flying colours! Woo hoo!!

Keep up the awesome work for your next challenge...

STACEY BROWN

Exercise: *Spin me a Tale!*
(Card #3)

STACEY BROWN

Time for card #3!

For this exercise you'll need to channel your inner storyteller! Be creative and let your imagination take the lead on this one.

Keep the card face down.

Grab your timer and set it for 15-45 seconds.

STACEY BROWN

Start your timer.

Close your eyes.

Breathe deeply in through your nose and out through your mouth, clearing your mind of all thought.

When the timer goes off, open your eyes, and turn the page to get your instructions.

Write a little story about what you see on the card.

Does the picture itself tell a clear story?

Does it give you a feeling about what might be happening?

Use your imagination to write a backstory for the card.

The woman on the unicorn is leaving something behind but in a good way like maybe her past. The unicorn is taking her to a better place where she is free. Shes ready to let go

STACEY BROWN

_____

_____

_____

_____

_____

_____

_____

_____

_____

_____

_____

_____

_____

_____

_____

_____

_____

When you are finished, turn the page!

STACEY BROWN

What did you discover about this card? Was your story about a person or object on your card or the scene itself? What was the overall feeling this card gave you? Was it positive or negative? And what does that mean to *you*?

This card gave me a positive feeling. Almost like patience. This card made me feel like there is something good to come

STACEY BROWN

Congratulations!

You just met your IG! Pretty cool AND pretty impressive how quickly you picked up on the conversation!

Through those 3 exercises, you are hopefully getting an idea of how your IG communicates with you through the use of tarot cards.

I think we are ready to kick it up a notch and apply our new skills!

Before we begin the next IG exercise, make sure to add the three cards you just used back into the deck. There is one last prep step to take care of...

STACEY BROWN

12 DECK ETIQUETTE –
Part Three:
Shuffle Mania!

STACEY BROWN

Do you play card games like Go Fish, War, Poker, or Spades?

How comfortable are you with shuffling those cards?

There are many different ways to shuffle a deck of cards. Tarot cards come in all shapes and sizes, but are typically larger than a traditional playing card deck.

Many are printed on thicker card stock than regular playing decks, making certain shuffling methods a challenge.

Some cards are "gilded" with a pretty gold or silver edging that makes them more delicate.

And many of them are graced with beautiful, full colour artwork and text. If you want the design to stay fresh, shuffling them in certain ways will create more "wear & tear" on your cards.

These differences often cause some confusion when trying to shuffle them up.

(There have been many people I've read for that are scared to touch the cards because they don't know how to shuffle. Fear not!! For I have a solution!!)

There is no right or wrong way to shuffle them up and infuse them with your energy, but some methods are more efficient than others! So here are some suggestions and tips:

Buffalo Shuffle – This is the most common way to shuffle. Take your deck in your Left Hand, face down into your palm. Bring your Right Hand under the deck. Slowly and gently drop the cards in random sections into your Right

Hand, allowing each new section to fall on top of the last. Continue this process until you feel the cards have been shuffled enough! Don't worry if the cards fall on the table or the floor. Just pick them back up and reshuffle 'em into the pile!

Energize Me! Shuffle – *(My personal fav!)* There are those who believe that the left side of our body is for receiving energy and information, and our right side is for giving them. This technique is the reverse of the Buffalo Shuffle. Take your deck in your Right Hand; face down into your palm. Bring your Left Hand under the deck. Slowly and gently drop the cards in random sections into your Left Hand, allowing each new section to fall on top of the last. Lather, Rinse & Repeat until you feel the cards are sufficiently shuffled!! Don't worry if the cards fall on the table or the floor. Just pick them back up and reshuffle 'em into the pile!

Pop on Top Shuffle – This one is super easy! Take your deck and divide it into several sections on a flat surface. Then restack all the sections randomly. Do this at least three times to make sure the cards have been shuffled enough.

Shuffling's not my thing! Shuffle - This one's fun! Take your deck and drop all the cards one by one, or in small sections, face down on a flat surface. Once all cards are on the table, take your hands and swirl them all around in no particular order. When you have made a sufficient enough mess of the cards, gather them all up into a single stack. Done and done!

Please note *about the below techniques: While two of the most popular, most commonly thought of ways to shuffle cards, the bridge and corner methods, are not always the most effective or desired way to shuffle certain Tarot decks. You will need to use your discretion.*

Kool Katz Card Bridge Shuffle – This is the fancy-schmancy way professional card players' shuffle, mixing all the cards with lightening speed like magic! Divide the deck into 2 even piles face down. Take the width edges and cover them with your thumbs, slightly bending the cards inwards, bring the edges of both piles close enough to overlap.   When ready, release the card piles, a card at a time from each hand in quick succession, making a magical display of a colourful bridge and puffs of wind!   Straighten them up. Lather, rinse & repeat until you feel like you've shuffled enough!

Corner Shuffle - Divide the deck into 2 even piles, face down. Take the width edge corners of each pile and cover them with your thumbs, slightly bending the cards inwards, bring the corners of both piles close enough to overlap. When ready, release the card piles, a card at a time from each hand in quick succession. Straighten them up. Lather, rinse & repeat until you feel like you've shuffled enough.

There are many other shuffling techniques out there...too many to list here. As always, go with what works best *FOR YOU.*

One quick little thing to mention... *sometimes when shuffling, a random card falls out. This is no mistake!! This is a clear message from your IG! This is your inner guidance giving you a bonus message so PAY ATTENTION!*

Place the card to the side and make sure you review it before you continue. Once you've received the message, you can add it back into the deck, or you can leave it out as part of your complete reading. Your choice!

We are in the home stretch now folks! Get ready to feel like a star...

13 READING.
The Cards: Spreads and Fu.

Now that your cards are good and shuffled, are you ready for the main event? Let's whip up your first IG Card Reading! Shuffle your deck and place it face down on your reading surface. (A good reading surface can be a table, flat pillow, floor, large book, or bed. The flatter and wider the surface, the easier it will be to read your spread.)

What's a "Spread"?

A Tarot spread is a way to lay out the cards to help you get specific answers to your questions.

There are countless spreads to choose from based on what guidance you seek; the most common spreads being the One Card, Three

Card & the Celtic Cross. For our purposes, I've chosen a helpful version of the Three Card spread to share with you.

This spread gets to the heart of the matter!
Heart (position 1),
Strength (position 2), and
Challenge/Opportunity (position 3).

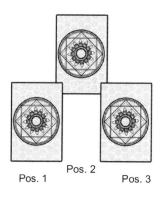

Pos. 2
Pos. 1   Pos. 3

With any spread, each card position answers a specific question. You want specific answers to your questions, right? Specific answers need specific questions! An appropriately formed, specifically worded question is *crucial* to helping you achieve *accurate guidance for your issues.*

Let's use a student of mine as an example. Vee has a problem. She has two best friends who like the same dude but neither of them have shared it with the other. They are both coming to her for advice. Vee doesn't know what to say or do. She feels caught in the middle and needs some IG help!

How can she word her questions to help her IG give her clarity?

 I might suggest Vee form her first question for <u>position 1</u> like this:

What is the *heart of the matter for me* in relation to my best friends' bizarre love triangle?

This cuts through all the confusing bits of an issue, shining a spotlight on the most important fact or driving emotion of what's going on, at the core.

Her second question for <u>position 2</u> is:

What are *my* strengths in relation to being a good friend to both?

What do I have going for me?

This question reveals what quality (qualities) Vee has within her to help her approach the issue with tact and grace, for the greatest success.

The third question for <u>position 3</u> might go something like this:

What opportunities or challenges **will I face** in relation to being a good friend to both?

This highlights perhaps the most important bit of guidance because it gives a tangible direction, road signs for what to be aware of or avoid, so she can be prepared and not caught off guard!

So what troubles you my dear? Tell me your problems... ;)

Now is a good time to come up with an issue you'd like your IG's advice on. Maybe it's boy or girl trouble. Maybe you are in a fight with a friend or the 'rents. Maybe you need help choosing your career path. Maybe you just want to know how to approach your math teacher about your dog eating your homework last night! Whatever your issue, getting the right wording is extremely helpful.

Why don't you give it a go? Using the above suggestion as a start off point, write questions to your specific issue.

_____

_____

_____

_____

_____

_____

_____

Got your questions? Groovy...Let's talk about the best ways to select your cards.

Grab your deck...

Exercise: *Choose, but choose...wisely!*

STACEY BROWN

There are many ways to choose your cards:

- With a prompted question, shuffling the cards until one falls or stands out to you,

- Randomly choosing from the deck,

- Choose the top three cards after shuffling.

There are no right or wrong ways to choose your cards here, as long as they remain FACE DOWN while choosing them! Go with what feels best to you. I'd like to share my favourite way:

STACEY BROWN

The FAN Method, with question prompts!

Place your shuffled deck, FACE DOWN, on a reading surface. Take your hand and fan them out so that most of the card edges are visible on one side.

Have your personal questions ready.

STACEY BROWN

The 1st card you are going to pull answers your first question: *What is the heart of the matter in relation to _____?*

Then pull a card from the fan with that question in mind. *Lay it **face down** in front of you.* This card is in Position 1.

(I like to keep my eyes closed, and feel my way to the right card. Sometimes I feel a heat coming off a particular card that way. Other times, I keep my eyes open and scan the fan of cards until one card stands out to me. Try out both ways to see if they feel right to you!)

The 2nd card pull answers the question: *What is my strength in relation to _____? What do I have going for me?*

Now pull your second card. *Lay it face down next to the first card* in front of you. This card is in Position 2.

STACEY BROWN

The 3rd card pull answers the question: *What challenge or opportunity do I need to see, prepare for or face in relation to* _____?

Pull your third card and *place it face down next to the other two* in front of you. This card is in Position 3. Gather the remaining cards and place them to the side.

STACEY BROWN

Grab your pen.

Start your timer again for 15-45 seconds.

(You know the drill by now!)

Close your eyes.

Breathe deeply in and out, clearing your mind of all thought.

When the timer goes off, open your eyes, and turn the page.

Flip over the Card in Position 1, asking yourself:

What is the heart of the matter I'm facing right now?

What is the first thing you notice when you look at the card?

You may get a word, an image, or a feeling about the card. Something you see, hear, feel, sense, smell or taste? Something you just know? What is the story on the card? What is it depicting? What does that mean for you?

Write down your responses.

_____

_____

_____

_____

_____

_____

_____

_____

_____

_____

_____

_____

_____

_____

_____

When you are ready, turn the page!

STACEY BROWN

Now flip over the 2nd card, asking yourself:

What is my strength in relation to this matter? (What do I have going for me?)

What is the first thing you notice when you look at the card?

You may get a word, an image, or a feeling about the card. Something you see, hear, feel, sense, smell or taste? Something you just know? What is the story on the card? What is it depicting? What does that mean for you?

STACEY BROWN

Write down your responses.

_____

_____

_____

_____

_____

_____

_____

_____

_____

_____

_____

_____

_____

_____

_____

When you are ready, turn the page!

STACEY BROWN

Now flip over the 3rd card.

What challenge or opportunity do I need to be aware of in relation to this matter?

What is the first thing you notice when you look at the card?

You may get a word, an image, or a feeling about the card. Something you see, hear, feel, sense, smell or taste? Something you just know? What is the story on the card? What is it depicting? What does that mean for you?

STACEY BROWN

Write down your responses.

_____

_____

_____

_____

_____

_____

_____

_____

_____

_____

_____

_____

_____

_____

When you are ready, turn the page!

So what does your IG have to say? Anything juicy?!;)

Looking at your spread (all three cards), can you give an overview of what your IG is telling you? How does each card and its message relate to your issue? Does it tell a story here or give straightforward wisdom? Pay close attention to how each card answers its prompt question. Your guidance lies there!!

_____

_____

_____

_____

_____

_____

_____

_____

_____

STACEY BROWN

_____

_____

_____

_____

_____

_____

_____

_____

Holy cannoli...pretty impressive!!   YOU DID
IT!!!

Congratulations! How do you feel?
(Pat yourself on the back!
Double pat!)

_____

_____

_____

_____

_____

_____

_____

_____

Holy cannoli...pretty impressive!!   YOU DID
IT!!!

Congratulations! How do you feel?
(Pat yourself on the back!
Double pat!)

STACEY BROWN

14 WHAT'S MY PRIMARY MODE OF RECEIVING?

STACEY BROWN

Well doesn't that sound technical?!! It's really not as complicated as it may sound...I promise! I'm not really a very technical girl. ;)

It is common for each person to have a Primary Mode of Receiving, the mode that your IG chooses to share messages and information with you through most often. This mode comes easiest to you, providing the most amount of information, without much effort. Think of it as a private language only you and your IG can speak and understand.

When you were completing the exercises, was there a sense or two that seemed to come more naturally or gave you information with more ease and detail than the others? Did you notice that you received all your information about the senses in the same way or differently?

Inner Guidance comes to everyone in different ways.

For some it's a very visual experience, seeing things in the mind like pictures on a blank canvas, like a movie playing, or like a hazy image or impression. This is referred to as *Clairvoyance.*

For others, their auditory skills are prominent, hearing things inside or outside their heads as voices, words and known sounds. This is called *Clairaudience.*

Others may feel the information as a physical sensation happening within their bodies, like chills and tingles, and even mimicking injuries and illnesses temporarily. This is known as *Clairsentience.*

Many sense things accurately about people, situations and environments around them constantly without a rational reason as to why. This is known as *Intuition* (aka Sixth Sense).

Some just know the information asked, and receive an answer from within. They've never formally learned the information. There is no concrete proof for what they know. They don't even have an explanation for how they know it. This is *Claircognizance*.

And there are those who receive this information through their sense of smell and taste, perhaps coming through as a memory of a perfume their grandma used to wear or the taste of apple pie at a fair. Exploring those memories hold messages their inner guidance wants them to know or relate to. These are referred to as *Clairalience* and *Clairgustance*.

Based on the above descriptions, what is your Primary Mode of Receiving?

_____

_____

And most of us also have anywhere from one to all of the modes to a lesser degree as Secondary Modes.

Any Secondary Modes?

_____

_____

_____

_____

_____

Before you fret, there is no mode better than the others! It's all about learning your Primary mode, how it works for you, and developing it so you have complete trust in its wisdom. (*You can also learn to develop your secondary modes, but that's a whole different book!!*)

15 FROM PADAWAN TO MASTER

STACEY BROWN

And look how far you've come!! By now, you have been formally introduced to your Inner Guidance AND had an insightful conversation, giving you clarity on an issue. You've also begun to establish your own personal language exchange, deciphering your inner code. Man, am I a good hostess with the mostest or what?!! ☺

So what's next? How can you get more confident in your IG chats?   Why, with practice of course! Even though we've thrown tradition out the window, there are some things that remain true across the board. "Practice makes perfect" applies.

The nice thing about practice for this subject is that it should be effortless! "Work" is not accompanied by "Hard" for once. In fact, you will only be able to tune into your IG when you are chill!

And become good friends, lifelong friends, with your IG. Get to know him, her, it, them – whatever floats your boat! Cultivate this friendship – the connection will be worth it.

So here's what I propose…

Make a commitment to use your cards 5 minutes daily for the next 7 days, following the exercises you learned in this book. As you become accustomed to the way you receive messages and information, your IG's guidance will increase, and get more specific. This builds up trust and confidence in your <u>In</u>ner Guidance, your <u>In</u>ner Voice, your <u>In</u>tuition.

Notice how it's all about the "<u>In</u>"?   That's because this guidance comes from with<u>in</u>…it's that personal alarm system *built in to YOU* to keep you safe and keep you following your Heart, your Dreams, your Highest Self, your Truth, your Core.

This practice will change the way you think, the way you approach every task, every decision, every choice in your life, if you go with it. Why? Being in communication with the real you, at all times, about those things that matter most, and following your IG means that life can be an exciting adventure instead of a fearful dark forest of the unknown! Life no longer happens *to* you. Instead it happens *FOR* you. IG gives you options, for-knowledge, choices; you may not otherwise know you have. And only you can truly know what is best for you.

Don't misunderstand me, I'm not supporting anarchy or encouraging you to start a riot against your parents and teachers or anything like that!! (Whoa Nellie…Don't make the protester signs just yet.)

What I *am* encouraging is trust and reliance on your inner guidance because it never steers you in the wrong direction. When something feels "off" or "icky" to you, even when others don't agree, **trust yourself,** trust that IG. You are so powerful and capable with this designer tool! It's there to guide you, so you might as well put it to good use!

STACEY BROWN

16 *GRATITUDE*

STACEY BROWN

One last thing before I let you get back to the business of life and living! ;)

Let's talk about gratitude.

As with anything that is given to you, it is customary, and often hugely appreciated, to say, "thank you" to the source/giver. Even though our Inner Guidance is within *us,* it's very important to acknowledge the information received with gratitude. You might feel foolish saying "Thanks" to yourself but trust me...it's the way to go! As you've learned many times throughout this book, there are many ways to make this happen. Try out a few different ways and ultimately choose what works best for you!

I call my Inner Guidance my "High Self" and my "Divine Dream Team". You can name yours whatever feels right for you. Have fun with it! Use your imagination.

Here's my way of saying "Thanks!"

"Hey IG! Hi there Divine Dream Team! Thanks so much for the clarity and perspective today. And thanks for your wisdom too. I'm so grateful to have choices!"

Then I pat myself on the back!

(Double pat!!!)

I also always use my imagination to send out butterflies into the world to bring clarity to all as a gift for the guidance. But that's just me!

Give it a whirl. Repeat after me:

Hey IG!

(Hey IG!)

Hi there Divine Dream Team!

(Hi there Divine Dream Team!)

Thanks so much

(Thanks so much)

for the clarity & perspective today.

(for the clarity & perspective today.)

And thanks for your wisdom too.

(And thanks for your wisdom too.)

I'm so grateful to have choices!

(I'm so grateful to have choices!)

Now pat yourself on the back!

(Double pat!!)

You have successfully given yourself an Amazing reading!

Great Job!

I hope you feel really good about what you accomplished...be proud of yourself.

Your IG is!

Buh Bye. The End!

17 HELPFUL GOODIES

STACEY BROWN

"Choices" Card Spread

If you are so inclined, here's a helpful tip you can try out for those times when you have a choice to make between two or more options.

Do a Three Card Spread just like you did in the Reading Time chapter, and assign one choice to the process. At the beginning of your first question, add the words: "If I choose _____,"

Here's how it looks.

Let's say you got two job offers.

One is working as a cashier at a busy fast food chain. They are offering flexibility in your schedule but you have to work at least 2 weekend shifts a month, which means you will have to miss out on your weekend club activity half the time. They pay $1/hr above minimum wage and offer extra shifts on occasion.

The other is doing office filing and reception work answering phones for a local accountant. The hours are set at Monday, Wednesday and Friday after school for 3 hours. No weekend work. They pay minimum wage and offer small bonuses twice a year based on a performance review.

Both have pro's and con's. What do you choose?

Grab you cards and follow the Reading Time exercise. Let's call the Cashier job **Choice A** and the Filing job **Choice B**.

With **Choice A** in mind, pull three cards using the question prompt method.

Card #1: If I choose **Choice A,** what is the heart of the matter for me in relation to this job?

Card #2: If I choose **Choice A**, what are my strengths in relation to this job?

Card #3: If I choose **Choice A**, what are my challenges or opportunities in relation to this job?

Then rinse, lather and repeat for **Choice B**. *Pull three more cards from the already shuffled deck.* You do not need to replace the Choice A cards and reshuffle.

Your IG will be thrilled to give you some food for thought on the best fit for you!

STACEY BROWN

18 *TAROT ME SILLY!*

STACEY BROWN

As you know by now, this book is not about Tarot itself. Rather, it's about connecting to your Inner Guidance using Tarot as a tool. For those of you interested in learning more about the history and structure of Tarot, here are some places to start, as promised!

Seventy-Eight Degrees of Wisdom: A Book of Tarot by Rachel Pollack

http://www.salemtarot.com/tarothistory.html

https://marygreer.wordpress.com/2011/07/19/what-every-newbie-tarot-reader-should-know-about-the-history-and-myths-of-tarot/

http://www.owlsdaughter.com/

Also, feel free to check out your local Metaphysical store for workshops and Tarot readers in your area. They can be great fun!

About the Author

Stacey Brown, The Black Feather Intuitive, has been highly intuitive her entire life. As a child, Divine Spirit came to her through dreams and visions, and a powerful sensitivity to energies, both in people and places. After years of pursuing many creative avenues to fulfill the spiritual yearning in her heart, her psychic abilities found a purpose and place to blossom.

"As a trained opera singer, I've used my voice to reach and teach kids, teens and adults alike for many years, and now I'm excited to use it in a different capacity: to help heal others! My life purpose is to help others find – and live – their highest and best lives. I'm honoured to help you find *your* truth!"

In addition to her Intuitive work with clients, she is a Certified Empowerment Coach, blogger of Feathers of Wisdom, Shadowbox artist, lecturer, author and recording artist of multiple guided meditations including *Creating Your Happy Place* and the Wings series featuring *On Butterfly Wings, On Bumblebee Wings* (both available on Amazon & iTunes)*, and On Phoenix Wings*. She lives in Morrisville, NC with her supportive husband, two beautiful stepdaughters, and two fur babies. She is currently working on her 2nd book.

STACEY BROWN

Other works by The Black Feather Intuitive:

Guided Meditations

On Butterfly Wings (Healing)

On Bumblebee Wings (Self Awareness)

On Phoenix Wings (Transformation)

Instant Vacation: Creating Your Happy Place

A Joy-Full Heart (Realignment)

Dream the Magic Within
Bedtime Guided Meditation for Kids

Books

Teen Superpower IG:
Demystify Your Inner Guidance using Tarot

Teen Superpower IG:
Demystifying Your Inner Guidance using Meditation
(Available Fall 2016)

To schedule a reading or coaching session, contact
Stacey directly. (Remote sessions available.) Please
visit her web site for contact information and updates.

www.blackfeatherintuition.com

STACEY BROWN

Notes:

STACEY BROWN

Notes:

STACEY BROWN

Notes:

STACEY BROWN

Notes:

STACEY BROWN

Notes:

94009327R10130

Made in the USA
Columbia, SC
21 April 2018